GX
POWER

GET YOUR GAME ON!

10,000	1,000	100
9,000	900	90
8,000	800	80
7,000	700	70
6,000	600	60
5,000	500	50
4,000	400	40
3,000	300	30
2,000	200	20
1,000	100	10

Or your opponent will!

Use beads or coins to keep track of your life points.

POJO.com
When it's not just a game!

TRIUMPH
B O O K S
542 South Dearborn Street, Suite 750
Chicago, Illinois 60605
www.triumphbooks.com

Table of Contents

Life Point Counters can be found at the front and back of this book!

Credits

Editor in Chief – Bill Gill, a.k.a. "Pojo"

Creative Director & Graphic Design – Jon Anderson, a.k.a. "JonnyO"

Project Manager – Bob Baker

Contributors – Jae Kim, Evan Vargas, Adam Povey, Michael Lucas, Ricky Riles, George Niederhofer, Alex Searcy, Mike Chacinski, Bryan Camareno, Forest Thomer, Baz Griffiths, and Amy Gill.

Yu-Gi-Oh! keeps changing every year. With our Pojo Guides, we try our best to keep you up-to-date about all the changes in the Yu-Gi-Oh! World.

This is our 9th Yu-Gi-Oh! book, and so much has changed since our last book. The original anime (cartoon), "Yu-Gi-Oh! Duel Monsters" is now over. No more new shows of it are being made. We have said goodbye to Yugi, Joey, Tristan, Tea & Seto. But, thanks to Yu-Gi-Oh! GX, the "Heart of the Cards' is living inside new characters like Jaden, Syrus, Alexis, Chumley and Chazz.

I like the new direction Yu-Gi-Oh! is going. Yu-Gi-Oh! GX adds a flavor of Harry Potter to the storyline. In Harry Potter the kids go to Hogwarts to become better wizards. In Yu-Gi-Oh! GX, the kids go to Seto Kaiba's Duel Academy to become better duelists. Harry Potter lives in the Gryffindor dorm. Jaden lives in Slifer Red. Harry's mean teacher is Professor Snape. Jaden's mean teacher is Dr. Crowler. There are many fun similarities.

Consider this book to be your Hogwarts ... er ... Pojo's Duelist Academy. We're going to have fun. We're going to test your brain. And we're going to teach you how to become an excellent duelist.

You can learn all about the Yu-Gi-Oh! anime inside these pages. We'll teach you the best cards to use in your deck. We'll teach you how to build fun decks and decks that win. Then we'll test your Word Search skills. We'll even test your Yu-Gi-Oh! GX airplane building abilities!

Enjoy!

Pojo

Pojo

Jaden's Elemental Hero Deck

By: Mike Chacinski

Jaden is the main character in the hit show Yu-Gi-Oh GX, and he runs a powerful Elemental Hero Deck.

No matter what happens, Jaden always seems to pull a win out of his hat. So how does this Slifer Red always manage to do it? Well, let's take a look at his deck and see what it looks like.

Jaden uses his favorite monsters in the **Elemental Heroes** to beat his opponents and win all his duels. He uses the magic of **Polymerization, Miracle Fusion and Fusion Gate** to summon his Fusions.

His favorite Elemental Hero would have to be **Avian**, his trusted sidekick and the one he summons as his opening move. **Avian** is the most versatile Hero, since he can use it to fuse into **Flame Wingman** and **Tempest,** two of the most powerful Elemental Heroes.

Jaden is well on his way to become the next "King of Games", even though he needs to study a little bit harder to get there.

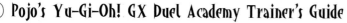

Jaden's Deck:

Elemental Hero Avian x2
Elemental Hero Burstinatrix x2
Elemental Hero Clayman x2
Elemental Hero Sparkman x2
Elemental Hero Bubbleman x2
Elemental Hero Wildheart x2
Elemental Hero Bladedge
Winged Kuriboh
Winged Kuriboh LV 10
Wroughtweiler
Dark Catapulter
Polymerization
Fusion Sage
The Warrior Returning Alive
Feather Shot
Transcendent Wings
Bubble Shuffle
Spark Blaster
Skyscraper x2
Burst Return
Bubble Blaster
Bubble Illusion
Monster Reborn

Fusion Gate
Miracle Fusion
A Hero Emerges
Draining Shield
Negate Attack
Hero Signal x2
Feather Wind
Clay Charge
Hero Barrier
Mirror Force

Fusion Cards:

Elemental
  Hero Thunder
  Giant
Elemental Hero
  Flame Wingman
Elemental Hero Tempest
Elemental Hero Rampart
  Blaster
Elemental Hero
  Shining Flare Wingman
Elemental Hero
  Wildedge

When in the classroom, Jaden usually does something that most of students think about doing: sleeping. But when it comes to dueling, Jaden is always at the top of his game and plays hard. He knows how to put his cards together and summon up his favorite Fusion monsters. Whether through a static blast by the **Thunder Giant** or a flame burst by the **Flame Wingman**, Jaden always gets his job done.

   Jaden plays more with his heart than his head. Too bad he can't put that kind of focus into his school work.

   Until next time, you know what Jaden always says…

Get Your Game On!

Dueling the Chazz Princeton Way!

**By: George Niederhofer
a.k.a. YamiBakuraFan**

C hazz is Jaden's main rival throughout the GX series. Once a stuck-up Obelisk Blue member, Chazz is now a member of Slifer Red and is always struggling to defeat Jaden and prove that he is the best! The deck Chazz uses is a mixture of many different card combos that focus around the **Ojama Trio, VWXYZ,** and **Armed Dragon** monsters.

Such a combination of deck types is nearly impossible to win with in the real world. So let us make an easy to use Chazz Deck.

In this deck, Armed Dragons and V-Z pieces are your main attackers. Ojamas can provide a quick stall or advantage with **Ojamagic**.

Discard **Fusilier Dragons** for **Armed Dragon**'s effect to destroy your opponent's monsters!

You can also power up **Fusilier Dragon** and any of the V-Z pieces with **Limiter Removal**. V to Z fusion cards will let you discard Ojamas and Ojamagics to

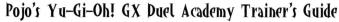

obtain more Ojamas to discard while getting off nasty effects that will cripple your opponents.

If you can get all three Ojamas onto the field, you can completely destroy your opponent with **Ojama Delta Hurricane!**

Obtaining the cards you want shouldn't be hard with **Magical Mallet** and **Card Destruction.** You can also use **Pot of Avarice** for combos with Armed Dragon, Ojamagic, and V to Z! This deck will say one thing to your opponent's cards: *"You. Go. Bye Bye!"* ■

Chazz Deck

1 x Armed Dragon Lv. 10
1 x Armed Dragon Lv. 7
2 x Armed Dragon Lv. 5
2 x Armed Dragon Lv. 3
2 x Fusilier Dragon
   – The Dual Mode Beast
1 x V-Tiger Jet
1 x W-Wing Catapult
1 x X-Head Cannon
1 x Y-Dragon Head
1 x Z-Metal Tank
2 x Ojama Green
2 x Ojama Yellow
2 x Ojama Black
1 x Sangan
2 x Magical Mallet
1 x Graceful Charity
1 x Card Destruction
1 x Limiter Removal
1 x Swords of Revealing
   Light
2 x Ojamagic
1 x Ojama Delta
   Hurricane!!
1 x Level Up!
1 x Pot of Avarice
1 x Premature Burial
1 x Snatch Steal
1 x Mystical Space
   Typhoon
1 x Heavy Storm
1 x Mirror Force
1 x Call of the Haunted
1 x Torrential Tribute
1 x Grave of Enkindling
1 x Ojama Trio

Jinzo's Supernatural Deck!

**By: George Niederhofer
a.k.a. YamiBakuraFan**

Jinzo is the villainous duel monster spirit that confronts Jaden and company in GX Episode # 14.

Jinzo was accidentally brought back to life by Torry and the Obelisk Blue séance club. But Jinzo is no friendly ghost!

Jinzo's deck is what I call a *Supernatural Deck*. A Supernatural Deck is based around combos that involve cards relating to ghosts, ghouls, and other cards of the supernatural world.

In the original Yu-Gi-Oh! series, *Yami Bakura* showed off his Supernatural deck that was based around **Dark Necrofear** and the **Destiny Board.** Jinzo's deck has all new combos that center around **Ectoplasmer,** a frightening card indeed. Ectoplasmer will constantly clear the duelist's field and inflict heavy damage to the opponent's life points. Jinzo uses all kinds of combos in his deck to abuse this card's effect to the fullest.

Jinzo's deck is structured around the use of many different combos and will keep your opponent on his toes!

When you sacrifice **Emissary of the Afterlife** with Ectoplasmer or when it's destroyed you can search out any of Jinzo's spooky zombie-type monsters! These zombies will not only be good on the offensive, but will be able to special summon back to the field over and over with the help of cards like **Book of Life, Spirit Caller,** and **Soul Resurrection.**

Card of Safe Return allows you to draw more cards every time a monster is special summoned from the graveyard. Since Jinzo's combos all specialize in monsters coming back from the grave, a well-placed Card of Safe Return will guarantee plenty of chances for free draws.

Jinzo's Supernatural Deck

- 1x *Jinzo*
- 3x *Malice Doll of Demise*
- 3x *Emissary of the Afterlife*
- 2x *Spirit Caller*
- 3x *Dragon Zombie*
- 3x *Armored Zombie*
- 3x *Clown Zombie*
- 1x *Sangan*
- 3x *Ectoplasmer*
- 2x *Book of Life*
- 2x *Card of Safe Return*
- 1x *Graceful Charity*
- 1x *Amplifier*
- 1x *Book of Moon*
- 1x *Snatch Steal*
- 1x *Premature Burial*
- 1x *Mystical Space Typhoon*
- 1x *Mirror Force*
- 1x *Call of the Haunted*
- 1x *Torrential Tribute*
- 1x *Spirit Barrier*
- 2x *Soul Resurrection*
- 2x *Sakuretsu Armor*

The final combo puts Jinzo himself into play, and with a little help from his personal favorite equip card, **Amplifier,** he will completely shut down all of his opponent's traps!

Jinzo's deck is structured around the use of many different combos and will keep your opponent on his toes! Only the bravest of duelists will dare duel with the lost souls that dwell within these cards. Who will be brave enough to use this deck? I'm sure you will want to give it a try! ■

Take Your Game to the Next Level!
Traditional Format vs. Advanced Format

By: Bryan Camareno

I'm sure that many of you have been to your local store and have seen kids playing in tournaments. Usually these kids will be playing by rules that you should learn.

The days of *"No Sacrifices"* are over. It's time to take your game to the next level.

There are two tournament formats in YuGiOh: Traditional and Advanced.

Traditional format is what most of you are probably used to. Traditional format has its own *Restricted List* of cards that you may use only 1 or 2 of in your decks. You may also recognize that this format allows

you to use powerful cards like **Black Luster Soldier – Envoy of the Beginning, Chaos Emperor Dragon – Envoy of the End, Raigeki, Yata-Garasu, Harpie's Feather Duster,** etc.

Advanced format has something called a *Forbidden List*. Some cards are so powerful (or unfair) that they are not allowed to be

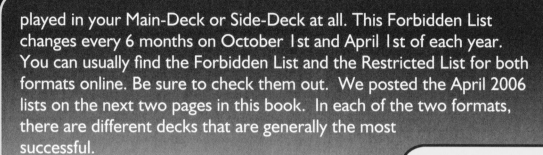

played in your Main-Deck or Side-Deck at all. This Forbidden List changes every 6 months on October 1st and April 1st of each year. You can usually find the Forbidden List and the Restricted List for both formats online. Be sure to check them out. We posted the April 2006 lists on the next two pages in this book. In each of the two formats, there are different decks that are generally the most successful.

Be sure to ask your Mom or Dad if it's alright for you to visit this website. Never, ever go to a new website without your parents' okay!!

In Traditional format these are the best decks:
- **Chaos Control**
- **Chaos Aggro**
- **Dark World**
- **Magical Scientist One-Turn Kill**

Here are the most successful decks in the Advanced Format right now:
- **Monarch Control**
- **Tomato Control**
- **Chaos/Return**
- **Flip-Flop Control**
- **Chaos Aggro**

If you are curious about what kind of cards these decks contain, go to www.pojo.com. At the top-right of the page and you will see the words **"Message Boards"**. Click on that to visit the forums and register to become a member. Search for the names of these decks and read up on what cards they use. This will help you learn about the structure of these decks and give you something to experiment with. ■

Until next time remember to play hard, think about your moves, and most importantly…

have fun!

About the Advanced and Traditional Format Lists

FORMATS - ADVANCED

If you want to play Yu-Gi-Oh! *"By the Rules"*, then you need to learn all about the **Banned & Restricted Lists.** These 2 Lists are filled with cards you **"CAN"** and **"CANNOT"** use.

These lists are updated *twice per year*. We have posted both the Traditional List and the Advanced Format List for you on these two pages.

Why did we make these Lists so small? Well, these two Banned and Restricted Lists change twice per year. There are a ton of cards on each list. We want to give you an idea of all the cards that are on the lists, but you should always get the newest lists from the Internet. That is where the newest lists are officially kept. The Internet Lists are the ones other kids are using in tournaments.

What!?! I can't use my Pot of Greed card!

Where can you get the newest lists? The official Yugioh Trading Card Game Site is at *www.yugioh-card.com*. This site is kid friendly, and is run by Konami. Konami makes the **Yu-Gi-Oh! Trading Card Game!** Ask your Mom or Dad to visit the site and print out the newest lists for you, and put the lists in your Trading Card Binders. The list is located in a section that is always titled: "Forbidden/Limited Cards".

If you want to be a great duelist, you have to always pay attention to these 2 lists, and build your decks within the rules that keep the game fun and fair.

ADVANCED FORMAT LIST
EFFECTIVE APRIL 1, 2006

I. Forbidden Cards
You CANNOT use these cards in your Deck or Side Deck:

· Black Luster Soldier - Envoy of The Beginning
· Butterfly Dagger - Elma
· Change of Heart
· Chaos Emperor Dragon - Envoy of The End
· Cyber Jar
· Dark Hole
· Delinquent Duo
· Exchange of The Spirit
· Fiber Jar
· Harpie's Feather Duster
· Imperial Order
· Last Turn
· Magical Scientist
· Makyura The Destructor
· Mirage Of Nightmare
· Monster Reborn
· Painful Choice
· Pot Of Greed
· Raigeki
· Ring Of Destruction
· Sinister Serpent
· The Forceful Sentry
· Time Seal
· Tribe-Infecting Virus
· Witch Of The Black Forest
· Yata-Garasu

II. Limited Cards
You can only use ONE of the following cards in the Deck & Side Deck combined:

· Book of Moon
· Breaker The Magical Warrior
· Call Of The Haunted
· Card Destruction
· Ceasefire
· Confiscation
· D. D. Assailant
· D. D. Warrior Lady
· Dark Magician Of Chaos
· Drop Off
· Exiled Force
· Exodia The Forbidden One
· Graceful Charity
· Heavy Storm
· Injection Fairy Lily
· Jinzo
· Last Will
· Left Arm Of The Forbidden One
· Left Leg Of The Forbidden One
· Level Limit - Area B
· Lightning Vortex
· Limiter Removal
· Mage Power
· Magic Cylinder
· Mask Of Darkness
· Metamorphosis
· Mirror Force

- Morphing Jar
- Mystical Space Typhoon
- *Night Assailant*
- Pot Of Avarice
- Premature Burial
- Protector Of The Sanctuary
- Reckless Greed
- Right Arm Of The Forbidden One
- Right Leg Of The Forbidden One

- Sacred Phoenix Of Nephthys
- *Sangan*
- Scapegoat
- Snatch Steal
- Swords Of Revealing Light
- Thousand-Eyes Restrict
- Torrential Tribute
- Treeborn Frog
- Tsukuyomi
- Twin-Headed Behemoth
- United We Stand

III. Semi-Limited Cards

You can only use TWO of the following cards in the Deck & Side Deck combined:

- Apprentice Magician
- Creature Swap
- Deck Devastation Virus
- Emergency Provisions
- Good Goblin Housekeeping
- *Gravity Bind*

- Magician Of Faith
- Manticore Of Darkness
- Nobleman Of Crossout
- Reflect Bounder
- *Reinforcement Of The Army*
- Upstart Goblin

TRADITIONAL FORMAT LIST
EFFECTIVE APRIL 1, 2006

I. Forbidden Cards

There are no Forbidden Cards in this format.

II. Limited Cards

You can only use ONE of the following cards in the Deck & Side Deck combined:

- Black Luster Soldier - Envoy Of The Beginning
- Book Of Moon
- Breaker The Magical Warrior
- Butterfly Dagger - Elma
- Call Of The Haunted
- *Card Destruction*
- Ceasefire
- Change Of Heart
- Chaos Emperor Dragon - Envoy Of The End
- Confiscation
- Cyber Jar
- D. D. Assailant D. D. Assailant
- D. D. Warrior Lady
- Dark Hole
- Dark Magician Of Chaos
- Delinquent Duo
- Drop Off
- Exchange Of The Spirit
- *Exiled Force*
- Exodia The Forbidden One
- Fiber Jar

- Graceful Charity
- *Harpie's Feather Duster*
- Heavy Storm
- Imperial Order
- Injection Fairy Lily
- Jinzo
- Last Turn
- Last Will
- Left Arm Of The Forbidden One
- Left Leg Of The Forbidden One
- Level Limit - Area B
- *Lightning Vortex*
- Limiter Removal
- Mage Power
- Magic Cylinder
- Magical Scientist
- Makyura The Destructor
- Mask Of Darkness
- Metamorphosis
- Mirage Of Nightmare
- Mirror Force
- *Monster Reborn*
- Morphing Jar
- Mystical Space Typhoon
- Night Assailant
- Painful Choice
- Pot Of Avarice

- Pot Of Greed
- Premature Burial
- Protector Of The Sanctuary
- *Raigeki*
- Reckless Greed
- Right Arm Of The Forbidden One
- Right Leg Of The Forbidden One
- Ring Of Destruction
- Sacred Phoenix Of Nephthys
- Sangan
- Scapegoat
- Sinister Serpent
- *Snatch Steal*
- Swords Of Revealing Light
- The Forceful Sentry
- Thousand-Eyes Restrict
- Time Seal
- Torrential Tribute
- Treeborn Frog
- Tribe-Infecting Virus
- Tsukuyomi
- Twin-Headed Behemoth
- United We Stand
- *Witch Of The Black Forest*
- Yata-Garasu

III. Semi-Limited Cards

You can only use TWO of the following cards in the Deck & Side Deck combined:

- Apprentice Magician
- Creature Swap
- Deck Devastation Virus
- Emergency Provisions
- Good Goblin Housekeeping
- Gravity Bind
- *Magician Of Faith*
- Manticore Of Darkness
- Nobleman Of Crossout
- Reflect Bounder
- Reinforcement Of The Army
- *Upstart Goblin*

The Top 30 Cards in the New Format

By: JAELOVE

A Hey guys, this is JAELOVE from Pojo.com. Earlier in this book we discussed the difference between the Traditional and Advanced Format. I think you and your friends should only be playing the Advanced Format. It is the most fun! It is also the most fair for everyone. Here is a list of the best 30 cards in the new Advanced format based on the April 2006 Advanced Format Banned & Restricted List.

1. Graceful Charity

There are only two cards in this format that allow you to draw through your deck Seeing more cards in your deck is always good, and this is the best way to do so!

2. Heavy Storm

You can't battle if your opponent uses too much defense. Use Heavy Storm to clear the backfield and get your monsters in for more damage.

3. Sangan

You can't hide from the fuzzy Sangan. He can attack directly, be tributed, or defend for almost no cost to your hand. He also finds some of the best cards in the game.

4. Breaker the Magical Warrior

The only reliable form of spell trap removal in monster form. It packs a powerful 1900 punch also, and it's a Dark monster for Chaos Sorcerer. Every single aggressive deck needs this card, which makes Breaker the only monster in the game that every attack-oriented deck should run.

5. Snatch Steal

Take your opponent's monster and add him to your army! A great card to use for victory.

6. Call of the Haunted

Being able to chain this card with options like Sangan or Jinzo and carry on the battle phase makes this one of the best cards in the game. Use it with your tribute monsters for even more fun.

7. Mirror Force

Most players will learn to play around it, but this is the best defensive trap in existence.

8. Mystical Space Typhoon

This card sets up attacks that let you then generate an extra advantage. It also stops many important cards that can ruin your strategy.

9. Spirit Reaper

This bad boy is still as good as it gets in the monster department.

10. Premature Burial

Especially in conjunction with Graceful Charity, this card can bring huge threats to the field and works wonderfully in general.

11. Confiscation

Seeing your opponent's hand is great, even at the cost of 1,000 life points.

12. Treeborn Frog

A huge card in this format, it can help you quite a bit to maintain some sort of field presence.

13. Torrential Tribute

While this card can still generate huge swings in your favor; it's a lot weaker than other traps because your opponent can simply summon a monster, cross yours out, and attack directly.

14. Nobleman of Crossout

Your opponent loses his face-down monster and also loses a normal summon. This is a great card.

15. Magician of Faith

The best cards in this game are spells, so it makes sense to run Magician of Faith.

16. Cyber Dragon

A great way to get an extra summon, it also beats down almost every normal summon monster in the game.

17. Gravekeeper's Spy

An immediate +1, provided they don't attack it with a high attack monster. It can hold off the field for quite a bit.

18. Scapegoat

Great to block against cards like Return from the Different Dimension.

19. D.D Warrior Lady

Great if you need Light monsters. It's not as awesome if you don't, but it still does stop Treeborn Frog and Spirit Reaper.

20. Chaos Sorcerer

You'll have to build a deck around this card to make it work, but it's still awesome.

21. D.D Assailant

If your opponent plays a lot of heavy hitters, or if you play Return from the Different Dimension, D.D Assailant is a great card to push damage.

22. Mystic Tomato

A great card to send monsters to the graveyard, search out a Sangan, or search out a Spirit Reaper. It helps you maintain field presence, and cancels with Dekoichi.

23. Dekoichi the Battlechanted Locomotive

A great way of dealing lots of damage with a floater. This card is a "1 for 1" trade with a solid body.

24. Pot of Avarice

This card is very tricky to use, but it's a nice card if you can figure out how to work it into your deck.

25. Jinzo

A dark monster that punishes your opponent for using too many traps. Jinzo effectively negates mass removal.

26. Royal Decree

This card punishes too many traps.

27. Tsukuyomi

Still a great card, even though it's a bit too slow for this faster format.

28. Exiled Force

A great option for removing face-down monsters.

29. Smashing Ground

This destroys your opponent's monster and ruins their normal summon. A great card.

30. Dust Tornado

You might want to use this against cards like "Return from a Different Dimension" that will destroy you if you're not prepared.

Yu-Gi-Oh! GX Starter Deck REVAMPED!

By: Evan Vargas

I'm sure every player was really excited when they opened up their Starter Deck for the first time.

If you are using your Starter Deck as your Main Deck, you probably already know that some of the cards inside aren't the best in the world. I'm here to help you shape up that Starter Deck!

The Yu-Gi-Oh! GX Starter Deck, seems to focus on supporting the *Elemental Heroes.* Let's tweak this deck to make it stronger.

Red Medicine is one of the worst cards ever made, simply because giving up one card to gain a meager 500 life points is a terrible waste. Instead of a card that can give you a few more life points, a better card could have been drawn, such as one that destroys a monster like *Sakuretsu Armor* or *Smashing Ground.*

Cards that barely affect the life points, such as *Ookazi*, should be dropped.

Other yucky cards are: *Castle Walls*, *Gazelle the King of Mythical Beasts*, and *Kuribo*.

With the bad cards taken away, new and better cards will need to take their place. I suggest you buy two GX Starter Decks, and combine them to make a much better deck.

You'll have multiple copies of the main *Elemental Heroes*, as well as other great support cards. This will aid the deck by giving the player more consistency.

The following deck list can almost be built just by purchasing a second Yu-Gi-Oh! GX Starter Deck and combining some of the cards:

Add-Ons: Once you get your hands on some of the Elemental Hero Fusion monsters, such as **Elemental Hero Flame Wingman** and **Elemental Hero Thunder Giant**, add in a couple copies of **Miracle Fusion** to summon some of the toughest Elemental Heroes yet! ∎

Monsters –19–
[3] *Elemental Hero Sparkman*
[3] *Elemental Hero Clayman*
[2] *Elemental Hero Burstinatrix*
[2] *Elemental Hero Avian*
[2] *Elemental Hero Bladedge*
[2] *Luster Dragon*
[2] *Skelengel*
[2] *Magician of Faith*
[1] *Trojan Horse*

Spells –12–
[1] *Graceful Charity*
[1] *Heavy Storm*
[1] *Mystical Space Typhoon*
[1] *Snatch Steal*
[1] *Premature Burial*
[1] *Brain Control*
[2] *Tribute to the Doomed*
[2] *Fissure*
[2] *Dark Factory of Mass Production*

Traps –9–
[1] *Magic Cylinder*
[1] *Ready For Intercepting*
[2] *Dust Tornado*
[2] *Jar of Greed*
[3] *Sakuretsu Armor*

Blinding Light Blue Eyes Ultimate Dragon Deck

By: Forest Thomer

We all have a favorite monster. Mine is the powerful Blue-Eyes White Dragon. Everything about this creature makes me love the game. It's a big monster whose attack points rival all other monsters. In a sense, Blue-Eyes White Dragon is the King of Yu-Gi-Oh.

But I think the best thing about him is that he has a fusion whose attack is a whopping 4500 points. Since we all love this game, and I know all of us enjoy smacking our opponent's Life Points for as much as possible, I have set out to demonstrate how to build a **Blue-Eyes Shining Dragon Deck.**

The first thing to understand when using this monster is that he is a *Fusion*. This means he costs us a lot of resources to summon.

Let's pretend resources are money to explain things better. Let's say you have five dollars ($5.00). Usually, the cooler toys cost you the most money. If you spend $3.00 on one toy, you now only have $2.00 to spend on something else. So, if you come across another toy that costs $4.00, you can not afford to buy it since you spent your money already. Yu-Gi-Oh is a game about using resources to the max. By using all of your cards (or money) in a failed attempt to summon a monster, you are forced to recover resources. (If you spend all of your $5.00 you now have to save more money and spend a longer amount of time getting something you want.)

Blue-Eyes Shining Dragon is a very cool monster, but he requires a lot of resources to pull out. Thus, a deck built around him should try and find cheaper avenues to summon him. It's like going to a Yard Sale to buy toys instead of going to an expensive supermarket.

This deck uses cards like **King of the Swamp** to search out key cards like **Polymerization** (so you can fusion summon 3 Blue-Eyes White Dragons). Plus, this card acts as a substitute to summon the almighty **Blue-Eyes Ultimate Dragon**, so if you only have two Blue-Eyes White Dragons in hand, you do not have to wait to summon his fusion. This deck also takes the concept of saving resources to a higher extent by using **Dragon's Mirror**, which allows you to summon your mighty dragon from the graveyard. That's kind of like giving your brother or sister an old toy from under your bed for his or her birthday present. You didn't forget about the kid, but instead of spending money on something new you took a smart approach and saved some money.

How to Use this Deck:

Gravekeeper's Spy, Magical Merchant, and **Morphing Jar** all act as ways of speeding up the summon of your Dragons. These cards slim the deck down and also help you keep *hand and field presence.* This means that you continue to develop field control at no actual cost.

(Kind of like saving your allowance every week. The longer you go without spending money, the more money you have in the future.)

After you summon your dragons, **My Body as a Shield** protects them from your opponent. Your opponent will be very unhappy if you summon these monsters out. **My Body as a Shield** stops all of their attempts to destroy your monsters. Once you get Blue-Eyes Shining Dragon out you should have complete control of the game. For one, you have a monster whose attack points can potentially be over 3,000. On top of that, any effect that targets him is negated, so if your opponent uses **Sakuretsu Armor** or **Snatch Steal** you do not lose your monster. But beware of cards like **Smashing Ground, Widespread Ruin,** or **Bottomless Trap Hole**: these cards do not target your monster, so they escape the effect and will rid the field of your Blue-Eyes Shining Dragon. Save your **My Body as a Shield** for such situations.

If you don't own all of the cards in the deck, 1900 point monsters like **Luster Dragon** and **Skilled Dark Magician** are good substitutes for cards like **D.D. Assailant** and **D.D. Warrior Lady**. Remember: the key to winning a duel is to outplay your opponent by having field control. Big monsters help you control the field.

Go ahead and smile whenever you summon these awesome monsters. Blue-Eyes White Dragon is *King!!!* ■

BEUD DECK
3x Blue-Eyes White Dragon
2x Blue-Eyes Shining Dragon
3x Gravekeeper's spy
3x King of the Swamp
1x Magical Merchant
1x Morphing Jar
1x Sangan
3x Spirit Reaper
1x Breaker the Magical Warrior
1x D.D. Warrior Lady
1x Archfiend Soldier
1x Heavy Storm
1x Pot of Avarice
1x Graceful Charity
1x Mystical Space Typhoon
2x Polymerization
1x Dragon's Mirror
1x Premature Burial
2x Smashing Ground
1x Swords of Revealing Light
2x My Body As a Shield
1x Nobleman of Crossout
1x Call of the Haunted
1x Mirror Force
1x Torrential Tribute
3x Sakuretsu Armor
2x Bottomless Trap Hole

Fusion Deck
3x Blue-Eyes Ultimate Dragon

The Search for the Forbidden One EXODIA!!!

By: Adam Povey (a.k.a. Ryoga)

This is a typical **Exodia** deck. To win, stall the game until **Emissary of the Afterlife** and **Jar of Greed** draw **Exodia**. Then shout, *"Exodia Obliterate!"* to drive your opponent mad. There are also cards like **Peten the Dark Clown** to thin out your deck.

Now, *surprise is everything*. Once your opponent sees an **Exodia** piece, he will do everything to destroy you quickly, so this deck has to *stall!* Things like **Gravity Bind** stop your opponent from attacking, but **Mystical Space Typhoon**, which everyone uses, easily stops these. Hence, we have a backup plan: monsters! **Peten** can block three attacks. **Mystic Tomato** absorbs attacks and summons the ultimate wall, **Spirit Reaper**. Remember, though, that most everyone is playing **Spirit Reaper**, so duelists are used to getting rid of it. It might be better to fetch **Sangan** or **Peten** to thin the deck.

Sakuretsu Armor deals with annoying monsters, like Spirit Reaper, trying to destroy your hand. As such, don't use **Sakuretsu** to stop damage to your life points unless it is the only way to keep you from losing the game. Save them for an evil monster, like **Mystic Swordsman LV2** attacking **Magical Merchant**.

Be careful with **Jar of Greed.** You could use it quickly to draw a card, but it's better to wait for your opponent to try and destroy it and chain with the Jar. This way, you gain since the Jar replaces itself and your opponent loses his card. Also remember: don't leave **Exodia** in the Graveyard where your opponent can get rid of it. Use **Pot of Avarice** and the **Dark Factory** to save your pieces.

Most of the cards in this deck can be found in starter decks. **Emissary of the Afterlife** and **Pot of Avarice** are more difficult to get since they are Super Rares. You should be able to trade for **Emissary** since only **Exodia** decks use it, but you'll have to save up for **Pot of Avarice.**

You should alter the deck to suit you. **The Shallow Grave** could get an extra use out of **Emissary** and **Sangan.** If you don't use them often, get rid of **Premature Burial**, since its only use is recycling them. You might add another **Spirit Reaper** or a pair of **Gravekeeper's Spy** if you have trouble stalling long enough. Overall, though, have fun. **Exodia** isn't the best deck in the world, but it is easy to use and is a great way win. ■

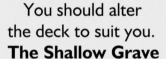

Deck (40 cards)

Monsters (20):
1 *Exodia the Forbidden One*
1 *Left Arm of the Forbidden One*
1 *Left Leg of the Forbidden One*
1 *Right Arm of the Forbidden One*
1 *Right Leg of the Forbidden One*
1 *Sangan*
3 *Emissary of the Afterlife*
3 *Peten the Dark Clown*
2 *Magical Merchant*
2 *Magician of Faith*
2 *Spirit Reaper*
2 *Mystic Tomato*

Spells (12):
1 *Level Limit – Area B*
1 *Graceful Charity*
1 *Premature Burial*
1 *Swords of Revealing Light*
1 *Scapegoat*
1 *Monster Reincarnation*
1 *Pot of Avarice*
1 *Book of Moon*
2 *Upstart Goblin*
2 *Dark Factory of Mass Production*

Traps (8):
2 *Gravity Bind*
3 *Sakuretsu Armor*
3 *Jar of Greed*

Tips for Trading and Collecting Yu-Gi-Oh Cards
Getting the Most BANG for Your Buck!

By: Michael Lucas

There are a LOT of Yu-Gi-Oh cards out there; thousands upon thousands of different cards are available to collectors and players alike. To younger or newer players, getting enough cards (or the right cards) to play can be a tough task. But there are some things you can do to get good cards, keep a good collection, and generally be an easier person to trade with. So here are a few tips that will help you to reach that point.

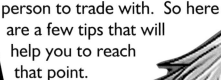

Buy in bulk

With many things in the world, if you buy more of something at one time, it ends up costing less than if you were to buy the items one at a time. Buying a box of cards (which usually costs around $60-70 for new sets) sure beats buying 24 packs at $4 each ($96). So instead of buying a pack or two every time you go to the store, save up and get a box when you have enough money. Not only will you get more cards, but you'll get at least a few foil cards. If you buy one or two packs at a time, you could get unlucky and pull no foils.

Know what your cards are worth!

In general, trading cards by their rarity is a good idea, but this isn't always the case. Some Super Rares are worth $2, and others $35. There are even some Normal Rare cards (like Dark Beginnings 2 Morphing Jar) that are worth more than even the Secret Rares from older sets! With prices being very low on some cards and high on others, a recent price guide would be a good thing to pick up.

For those of you with internet access, you can check out the popular shopping sites to see what cards are selling for. You don't need to buy anything to look up names of cards and see what people are selling them for; a minute or two of comparing prices can make sure you don't accidentally trade a $30 card for a $3 one.

Sort your collection!

I've been shown a lot of trade binders by a lot of players. Some have been sorted so well that even without seeing the binder before, I knew exactly where to look to check if the player had the card I needed. Others had cards spread out so far, I had to flip through over a hundred pages of cards to see if there was anything I wanted to trade.

My advice is to pick a method of sorting your cards and stick with it. Usually, it's best to take all the cards of a certain rarity (all Ultra Rares, then all Super Rares, then all Rares) and sort them by name, each in their own section of your binder. This will help people find what they're looking for quickly when trading with you, and it will help you find what you're looking for when you want to take a card out for your deck.

Special collections

For collecting, I leave with this one last idea: most players tend to have a favorite card and collect as many copies or different versions of it as they can. This is usually a good thing, especially if the card isn't widely wanted by a lot of other players. Having five full pages in a trade binder of your favorite card is impressive by any standards, and fun to show off to others. If nothing else, it'll give you a sense of accomplishment when you get your 10th, 20th, 50th, or even 100th copy of a card.

Hopefully, these tips will help some newer players avoid some of the common mistakes that most players make when starting out card games for the first time. Above all else, remember that Yu-Gi-Oh is still just a game:

Have fun with it!

Yu-Gi-Oh GX Character Bios

By: Baz Griffiths, George Niederhofer and Bill Gill

With the first season of Yu-Gi-Oh! GX coming to a close, we have met quite a few of the colorful characters residing in Duel Academy. Throughout this season, Jaden Yuki and company have faced many tough challenges and strong opponents. Season Two is just around the corner, so be sure to meet the cast.

Meet the cast

Jaden Yuki

Jaden is a confident duelist with a strong fighting spirit, but he was put into Slifer Red after humiliating Dr Crowler. Despite this, Jaden is determined to become the best duelist in the world, just like Yugi before him. His close bond with his friends helps him through the hard times; however, his tendency to break rules sometimes gets him in trouble.

Alexis Rhodes

Alexis is the most talented female duelist in all of Duel Academy. She is a top-notch player who resides in the Obelisk Blue dorm. Alexis shares a close friendship with Jaden. She is an independent thinker but prefers to do things by the rules. When her own brother Atticus disappeared from the academy, Alexis developed a strong sisterly bond with Zane.

Syrus Truesdale

Syrus and Jaden formed a strong friendship when they met during the entrance exams, and Syrus thinks of Jaden as his big brother. Syrus has the potential to be a strong duelist but lacks confidence in his own abilities. Syrus' older brother, Zane, is the strongest duelist in Duel Academy, and Syrus feels hidden in his brother's mighty shadow. Hopefully, sharing a room with Jaden will allow him to gain the skills he needs to progress as a duelist.

Chumley Huffington

Chumley failed his first year exams last year and was forced to retake the year. He is an optimistic person and his Australian-themed deck has potential; however, he never seems to be able to win when it really matters. After his duel with Dr. Crowler, Chumley pursued his goal and became a card designer for *Industrial Illusions*. He works for the game's creator, Maximillion Pegasus, and has left Duel Academy. Jaden and friends most likely haven't seen the last of their grilled-cheese-loving friend, though.

Bastion Misawa

Bastion was one of the strongest duelists in this year's entrance exam and was placed into the Ra Yellow dorm as a result. Never one to be at a disadvantage in a duel, Bastion has constructed six decks to meet every challenge. Bastion is a dueling genius and calculates theories on how to defeat his opponents before he actually duels them. While he is much stronger than most of his fellow students, the only person he cares about beating is Jaden.

Chazz Princeton

The youngest of three brothers, Chazz is a student who believed that only the best should be admitted into the academy, but his loss to both Jaden and Bastion caused him to rethink his attitude towards the game and other people. Chazz became the best duelist in North Academy and challenged Jaden to a rematch in the School Duel. After a third defeat, Chazz rejoined Duel Academy as a member of Slifer Red and started from scratch. Chazz is still Jaden's rival and longs to one day defeat Jaden.

Zane Truesdale

Zane is Syrus' brother and top of the third year class. Although Zane acts cold to his brother, he is just trying to make him stronger and is in reality a very kind and loving brother. His strong performance means that few are able to rival him, let alone defeat him, and many say he has achieved perfection. Jaden and Zane had a decisive battle in the Graduation duel and Zane finally left Duel Academy behind. Zane is now entering the pro dueling circuit, where he will face greater challenges then he ever imagined back on campus.

THE GX ANIMÉ - CHARACTERS

Dr Vellian Crowler

Dr Crowler is the head of the Obelisk Blue dorm. He believes that the Duel Academy should only allow in the very best students. Crowler has a dislike for slackers like Jaden and Syrus, but has lately begun to take a liking to them. When the Seven Shadow Riders attacked Duel Academy, Crowler showed his heroic side when he stood up for all of his students, even his least favorite ones.

Lyman Banner

Lyman is one of the teachers attached to the Slifer Red dorm. Hiding a secret identity, Lyman is actually one of the Seven Shadow Riders. His true identity is Amnael, an alchemist who wishes to obtain the three Sacred Beast cards in order to gain immortality. Amnael has been testing Jaden from the shadows throughout the series, resulting in Jaden's becoming a stronger duelist.

Atticus Rhodes

Atticus is Alexis' brother. He was taken into the abandoned dorms and brainwashed into the former Nightshroud to help obtain the spirit gate keys. He is a goofy guy who is loved by the ladies. Atticus enjoys helping Alexis with her love life. Atticus lives among the Obelisk Blue ranks and is second only to Zane.

Chancellor Shepard

Chancellor Shepard is the head of Duel Academy. He is called whenever things go wrong. Sheppard is in charge of hiding the spirit gate keys that keep the Legendary Beasts sealed underneath Duel Academy's surface.

Let the Classes Begin!

By: Baz Griffiths

This is a summary of the important parts of the first year of Yu-Gi-Oh! GX. It does not include information on episodes that do not effect the overall storyline.

A As each new year begins, **Seto Kaiba's Duel Academy** holds entrance exams to find the best duelists from around the land. Running late for his exam, **Jaden Yuki** accidentally bumps into **Yugi Moto** on his way to the Academy. Yugi offers Jaden a card that he hopes will bring him luck – *Winged Kuriboh.*

Jaden starts school with a duel against **Dr Crowler,** the head of **Obelisk Blue.** He also meets two other students – **Syrus Truesdale** and **Bastion Misawa.** Bastion's great skills got him into the **Ra Yellow** dorm. Syrus' weak performance and Jaden's humiliation of Dr Crowler mean they are put into the **Slifer Red** dorm with the drop out students.

In their new home, Jaden and Syrus meet their roommate **Chumley Huffington.** The three quickly become friends. Determined to prove himself as a duelist, Jaden declares that he will do whatever it takes to become the best in the year. However, his determination and skill cause problems with Obelisk Blue student **Chazz Princeton.** Jaden and Chazz quickly become rivals.

It is discovered that Titan was hired by Crowler in an attempt to get rid of Jaden.

When Jaden and the others hear rumors of a *haunted dorm*, they decide to investigate. They meet **Alexis Rhodes.** Alexis explains that her brother was one of the people who once went missing from the dorm. She wants to know what happened to him. Investigating the building, Jaden is challenged by the mysterious **Titan** to a shadow duel. Discovering that Titan's powers are all an *illusion*, Jaden is able to defeat him. It is discovered that Titan was hired by Crowler in an attempt to get rid of Jaden.

Chazz loses a duel to Jaden. Then Chazz is told that he must defeat Bastion to stay in Obelisk Blue. Chazz suggests that the loser of the duel must leave the academy. Using a *water deck* against Chazz's *fire* one, Bastion wins the duel easily. Chazz leaves the Duel Academy.

As the annual duel between the Duel Academy and the **North Academy** approaches, Jaden and Bastion must duel each other to decide who will represent the academy. Jaden wins, proving that he is a stronger duelist than Bastion.

Elsewhere, Chazz finds himself washed ashore on an island where he meets a mysterious old man. He takes Chazz to the North Academy where he will be able to train, and build a new deck. Chazz is chosen to represent North Academy in its duel against the Duel Academy.

When North Academy arrives for the duel, Jaden and the others are stunned to discover that the North Academy's representative is Chazz. Although Chazz is much stronger than before, he is still unable to defeat Jaden. Realizing that he still has a lot to learn, Chazz decides

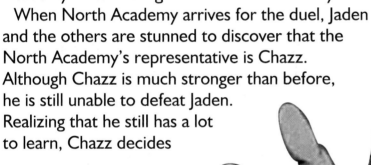

to remain at the Duel Academy, but he is surprised when he hears he will have to drop down to Slifer Red because he has missed three months of lessons.

The Seven Stars

Lyman Banner decides to take his Slifer Red class on a field trip to nearby ruins, and Alexis tags along, hoping that the ruins may hold some answers to her brother's disappearance. The group ends up trapped in a shadow world. Jaden wins a *mysterious pendant* from the grave keeper, which secures the safe return of his friends.

Jaden, Alexis, Bastion, Zane and Chazz are called to the principal's office. They are told that **three Legendary Beast cards** are sealed on the island, protected by seven spirit keys. The Principal gives the keys to Lyman, Crowler and the gathered students.

THE GX ANIMÉ - SEASON ONE

The Principal warns them that seven powerful duelists – **The Seven Shadow Riders** – are approaching the island in search of the spirit keys. The only way for the Shadow Riders to take the keys is to win them in a duel, so each duelist must do his or her best to protect their key.

Nightshroud, the first of the stars, challenges Jaden to a shadow duel atop a volcano. Jaden is able to defeat Nightshroud, but the stress of the shadow duel leaves him weak. Nightshroud also collapses at the end of the duel. Alexis learns that Nightshroud is actually her missing brother, **Atticus**.

The second Shadow Rider, **Camula**, arrives to claim the keys. Camula easily defeats Dr. Crowler in a duel. Zane then challenges Camula. Camula's *vampire deck* defeats Zane as well.

With two keys lost to Camula, Atticus warns Alexis that Camula is the worst of the Shadow Riders and that only somebody with a Shadow Item, such as Jaden's mysterious pendant, can defeat her. Using the pendant he received from the grave keeper, Jaden is able to counter Camula's shadow power and finally defeats her.

Bastion is challenged to duel **Taniya**, the third Shadow Rider. Bastion starts well, but he is distracted by her constant flirting and loses the duel. Jaden then challenges Taniya. Jaden narrowly defeats the third Shadow Rider.

The remaining keys are stolen by a group of bandits, and Chazz must duel the group's leader and the fourth Shadow Rider, **Don Zaloog**, in order to claim them back. Jaden is then confronted by the fifth Shadow Rider, the **Pharaoh Abidos the Third**, and once again protects his key.

Alexis is kidnapped by Titan and taken to the dorm where he lost to Jaden. Titan reveals that he now has real shadow powers and he is the *Sixth* Shadow Rider. Titan challenges Alexis to a duel. Alexis defeats Titan with some more support from her brother Atticus. Atticus tells Alexis that he was sent to the dorm by Lyman Banner and then kidnapped into the shadow world.

As Jaden and the others try to make sense of Atticus' revelations, Lyman mysteriously vanishes. Jaden and the gang realize that Lyman is actually the last Shadow Rider - ***Amnael!*** Separating to look for Lyman, Alexis and Chazz are both defeated by Amnael.

Amnael then challenges Jaden for the last key. As their duel goes on, Amnael reveals that he became ill many years ago and used a fake body - Lyman - to stay alive. Jaden defeats Amnael, the last of the Shadow Riders.

Alexis is shocked when Titan kidnaps her and takes her to the dorm where he lost to Jaden.

A volcano on the island begins to erupt. And the gates that release the Power of the Beasts start to open. Jaden and the group are confronted by the academy's former chairman, **Kagemaru.** Kagemaru challenges Jaden to one last duel which will fully awaken the power of the Beasts. Realizing that Lyman sensed this would happen; Jaden puts his *Philosopher's Stone* card into his deck.

Pojo's Yu-Gi-Oh! GX Duel Academy Trainer's Guide (49)

Although the duel is tough, Jaden's faith in the strength of his deck pulls through. Jaden defeats Kagemaru, once again sealing away the Legendary Beasts.

After everything else that has come their way, Jaden and the others still have one

final challenge to face – final exams. Chumley is told that he has won a contest and can become a *card designer,* but only if he proves himself in the practical exam. Facing Crowler in the final duel, Chumley puts all his faith in his *Australia-based deck* and manages the best performance of his life. Although he is eventually defeated by Crowler, the professor allows Chumley to take the card designer position anyway, saying that Chumley has made great progress over the last year.

With graduation approaching, the third year grades reveal that Zane is top of the class with full marks. Asked to choose his opponent for the exhibition duel at the end of the year, Zane asks that Jaden duel him in his final duel at the academy. The duel between the pair is close, eventually ending in a tie. Zane thanks Jaden for such a strong performance. Zane tells Jaden that he has no concerns about the future of the academy. ■

Year Two A Whole New Duel!

Season 2 preview

By: Baz Griffiths

With the new year at Duel Academy starting, all kinds of new duelists arrive and Jaden just can't wait to face them! Among these students is the mysterious **Aster Phoenix.** Aster is a pro duelist who uses the **Elemental Heroes** just like Jaden. After defeating Zane, Aster sets his sights on Jaden. After a clash of Elemental Heroes, Aster reveals his true trump set, a new set of cards called **Destiny Heroes** that surpasses the power of the Elemental Heroes. What are Aster's true motives? What are the motives of the mysterious man controlling him from behind the scenes? Stay tuned to find out. ■

Review of Yugioh World Championship: Ultimate Masters
For the Game Boy Advance

By: Alex Searcy

This is by far the best World Championship game to date.

In the beginning of the game, as a Starter Deck, you get to choose any one of the current **Structure Decks**, from Fire all the way to the newest *Spellcaster* Structure Deck.

You begin with five duelists available to duel. All your opponents are monster cards or tokens.

Once you defeat each duelist on a level, you unlock another level of duelists. If you defeat an entire row three times (or five, depending on where your card level is), you unlock a new booster.

It's cool that you can choose your own Avatar, and can even change it if you want. You can also participate in Theme Duels and Survivor Matches, which unlock as you progress in the game. However, you must complete up to 95% of the Duel Puzzles

in order to successfully unlock each duelist in the fifth and final level.

Getting New Cards

Each duelist you defeat, gives you DP (Duelist Points), which you use to purchase new cards. In the beginning, you start off with several boosters from the **Legend of Blue Eyes** set up to **Ancient Sanctuary.**

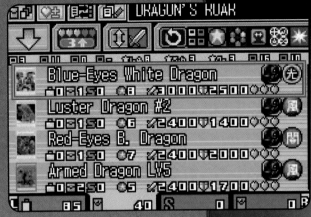

As the packs progress, they cost more DP. Legend of Blue Eyes is only 150 DP but Ancient Sanctuary is 350 DP. As you unlock new boosters up to **Shadow of Infinity**, which costs 500 DP, you can get cards that are powerful to help you build an even better deck.

You get DP for losing as well, but your total is divided by ten, so you usually are lucky to get 50 DP or so from a loss, but you can get up to 1500 or 2000 DP if you win a duel.

You can also unlock Special

Boosters that specifically contain certain types of cards, and only that type. I find this game rather good and recommend purchasing it. ∎

Review of Yugioh GX Duel Academy
Game Boy Advance

By: Alex Searcy

Would you like to rise to the rank of **"The King of Games?"** I know I would, and I'm sure you would as well, but this game won't take you there. Honestly, I found this game somewhat disappointing.

This game is a lot like the Yugioh GX television show. You start off at *Duel Academy,* and you can choose whether you're a boy or a girl.

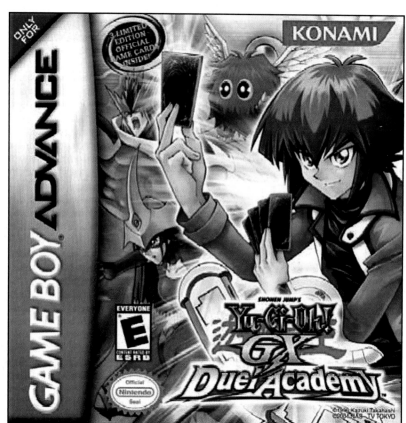

You start of the game as a *Slifer Red,* but you can progress by winning certain challenges.

You take actual classes and every so often, you must take an exam. To advance to the next class level (*e.g. Slifer Red to Ra Yellow; and then Ra Yellow to Obelisk Blue),* you must also complete certain tasks.

Yugioh GX main characters are involved in this game and their decks are nearly identical to the television show. People like **Alexis, Bastian, Chazz, Doctor Crowler, Professor Banner,** and even **Jaden** are available.

Sometimes you have to fulfill specific tasks, and you can duel the main characters. Other times when you complete tasks for characters, they give you a certain card (or cards).

As for acquiring other cards, you still acquire DP or Duel Points for your victory over your opponents. You then can buy *random* packs of cards. The packs have random **Monster/Magic/Trap** pictures on the front. It is very difficult to find cards you may want, despite the pack picture(s). This is frustrating!

I do not like this game as much as the Ultimate Masters game I reviewed on pages 52 and 53. It can be fun at times, but it is frustrating to get all the cards you really want. ■

Dungeon Dice Monsters

DDM Board with game peices

Starter Box

Booster Pack

By: TheDungeonMaster

You may have seen **Dungeon Dice Monsters** played in the *Yu-gi-oh!* anime on television. Yugi battled Duke Devlin for a few episodes. But did you know that you could play this game at home? Mattel made this game for a few years. You can still find the starter boxes and booster packs if you search hard enough.

Dungeon Dice Monsters is a game played using dice and monsters figures. You get a team of monsters and you try to summon them into the Dungeon. Your monsters then battle against your opponent's monsters inside the dungeon. When your monsters get to the other side of the Dungeon, they get to attack your opponent. When they hit your opponent 3 times, you win.

How do you summon the monsters?

You have dice. That's why it's called Dungeon *DICE* Monsters. There are four different types of dice. You and your opponent take turns rolling dice. If you get two of the same summoning, you can summon a monster. If you get two *Level 2 Summon* dice, then you can summon a level 2 monster. Same with level 3 and 4. The larger numbers are stronger monsters, which are harder to summon to the dungeon.

What are the crests?

Summon - *Summons your monsters to the Dungeon*

Movement - *Allows your monsters to move in the Dungeon*

Trap and Spell - *Allows your monsters to use their special abilities.*

Attack - *Allows your monsters to attack*

Defense - *Allows your monsters to build up a defense against attacks*

The game gets interesting when both you and your opponent both start getting monsters in the dungeon and start to battle each other. The game is actually pretty simple and very fun. The monster figures are very cool too. Pick it up and give it a try! ■

DDM Cards

ANSATSU

LEVEL 2

⊕x3 This monster can stop one opposing monster's Special Ability when the opposing monster uses it. This only works against the [...] you will have to [...] to affect [...]

Warrior

GEARFRIED THE IRON KNIGHT

LEVEL 2

⊕x3 This effect only works when your Monster Lord gets attacked. Sacrifice this monster during one turn, and your Monster Lord won't receive any damage [...] turn ends.
[...] a Defense Crest, this [...] self.

Warrior

⚔40 / 🛡30

DARK MAGICIAN GIRL

LEVEL 2

② Add one Magic Crest to your Crest Counter.

Dark

HP:20 / ⚔20 / 🛡20

KNIGHT OF TWIN SWORDS

LEVEL 2

↑ Knight of Twin Swords can move 2 squares for each Progress Crest spent. When this monster performs this effect, he can't make a regular movement.

✗x2 This monster can perform two attacks against one monster for every two Attack Crests spent. To use this effect, an even number of Attack Crests must always be spent; however, this monster does not have to use all of its attacks.

Warrior

HP:30 / ⚔20 / 🛡10

Monster figures

Yugioh GX Word Search

Find these Yu-Gi-Oh! GX words in the Puzzle on the next page. Then, when your done, you can cut that page out and follow the GX instructions below to make your own Avian Flyer!

ABIDOS
ALEXIS
AMNAEL
ASTER PHOENIX
ATTICUS
BASTION
CAMULA
CHAZZ

CHUMLEY
DON ZALOOG
DR CROWLER
JADEN
KAGEMARU
LYMAN
NIGHTSHROUD

OBELISK BLUE
RA YELLOW
SHEPARD
SLIFER RED
SYRUS

TANIYA
TITAN
ZANE

Make Your Own Avian Flyer and Jaden Jet!

After you complete each puzzle on the next few pages, you can carefully cut out both your Avian Flyer and your Jaden Jet following the dotted line around the outside edge of each page. Then you're ready to follow the instructions on this page to fold your flyers and soar with Avian and Jaden!

Answers to Quiz on Page 61:
1.C; 2.B; 3.C; 4.A; 5.B

Plane Folding Instructions:

1. PUZZLE side up. Fold the page in half along Line 1.

2. Open the paper up again. Fold down corners A and B towards you so that they meet at the center fold.

3. Now fold the triangle made by A & B down the blank side.

4. Take corners C and D and fold them in towards the center of the page until their points touch E and F respectively.

5. This is what you should have so far - the printed side is now showing.

6. Now fold up the little triangle marked "FLAP" so that it covers (and "locks") corners C & D.

7. Fold the paper back in half along Line 1. And you're almost there!

8. Now fold down the "wings" along Lines 4 & 5 so that the tow halves of the face meet.

You're ready to fly!

Yugioh GX Word Search

```
A  C  B  O  D  G  N  Z  D  U  U  X  R  A  O  D
B  Z  A  R  X  O  Y  O  A  R  K  E  V  T  B  U
I  I  P  M  I  I  N  S  A  N  L  J  S  T  E  O
D  J  L  T  U  Z  N  M  O  W  E  H  A  I  L  R
O  B  S  A  A  L  E  E  O  N  E  L  Y  C  I  H
S  A  H  L  G  G  A  R  O  P  T  B  I  U  S  S
B  U  O  H  A  H  C  Q  A  H  U  C  N  S  K  T
N  O  G  K  I  R  M  R  N  R  P  Z  A  G  B  H
G  T  Y  B  D  U  D  Y  J  A  A  R  T  K  L  G
D  E  R  R  E  F  I  L  S  Y  L  M  E  G  U  I
N  A  M  Y  L  M  Z  D  L  E  E  S  B  T  E  N
Y  E  L  M  U  H  C  E  T  L  X  Z  Y  N  S  C
Z  Z  A  H  C  H  A  I  P  L  I  N  E  R  C  A
R  O  V  C  B  N  T  H  F  O  S  D  N  K  U  U
G  W  C  R  M  A  U  A  R  W  A  I  B  N  J  S
Q  E  J  A  N  N  M  X  R  J  R  A  K  Z  I  T
```

Cut away extra along this line before you start folding.

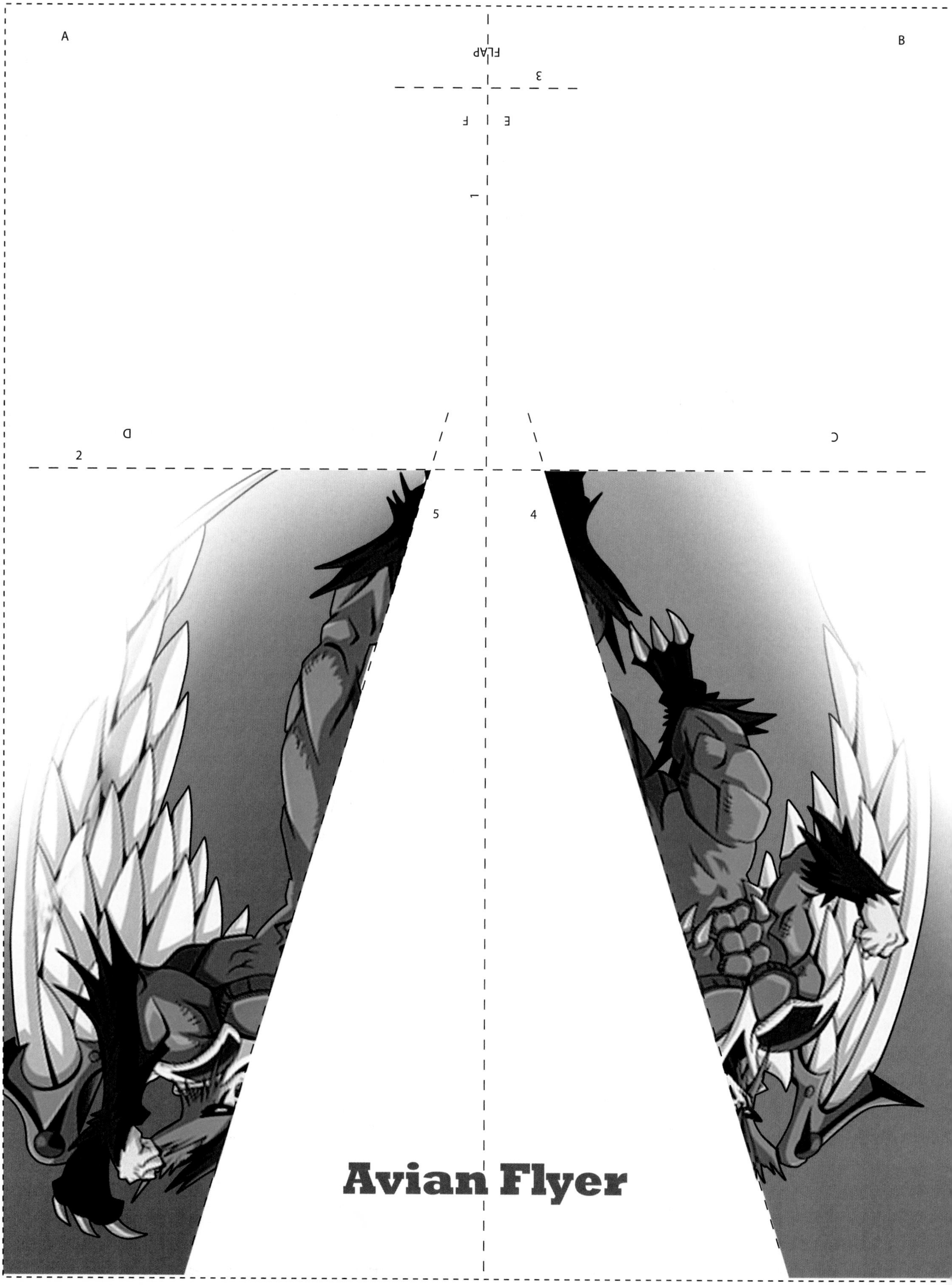
A
B
FLAP
3
E
F
1
D
2
C
5
4
Avian Flyer

Yugioh GX Quiz

Test your GX knowledge. Do *you* know enough about GX to be the *King of Games*?

1. Which characters from the original "Duel Monsters" series duel Jaden and Syrus?

      A: Marik and Ishizu   B: Yugi and Joey

      C: The Paradox Brothers   D: Pegasus & Kaiba

2. What does Chumley Huffington's father manufacture?

      A: Duel Monsters Cards   B: Hot sauce

      C: Duel discs   D: Fake Egyptian Artifacts

3. What card does Jaden get from Yugi in the first episode?

      A: Dark Magician Girl   B: Winged Dragon of Ra

      C: Winged Kuriboh   D: Dark Magician

4. Who founded Duel Academy?

      A: Seto Kaiba   B: Maximillian Pegasus

      C: Yugi's Grandfather Solomon   D: Arthur Hawkins

5. Who is the first person on the show to defeat Jaden?

      A: Dr. Crowler   B: Zane Truesdale

      C: Bastion Misawa   D: Chazz Princeton

Answers on page 58.

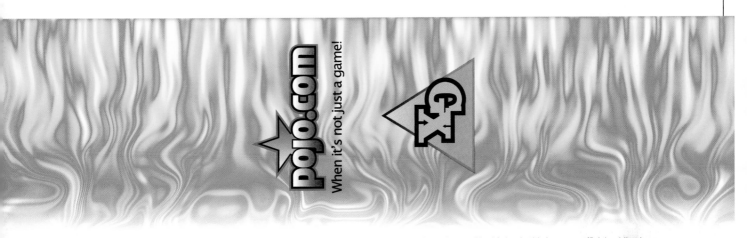

POJO.com

When it's not just a game!

Cut away extra along this line before you start folding.

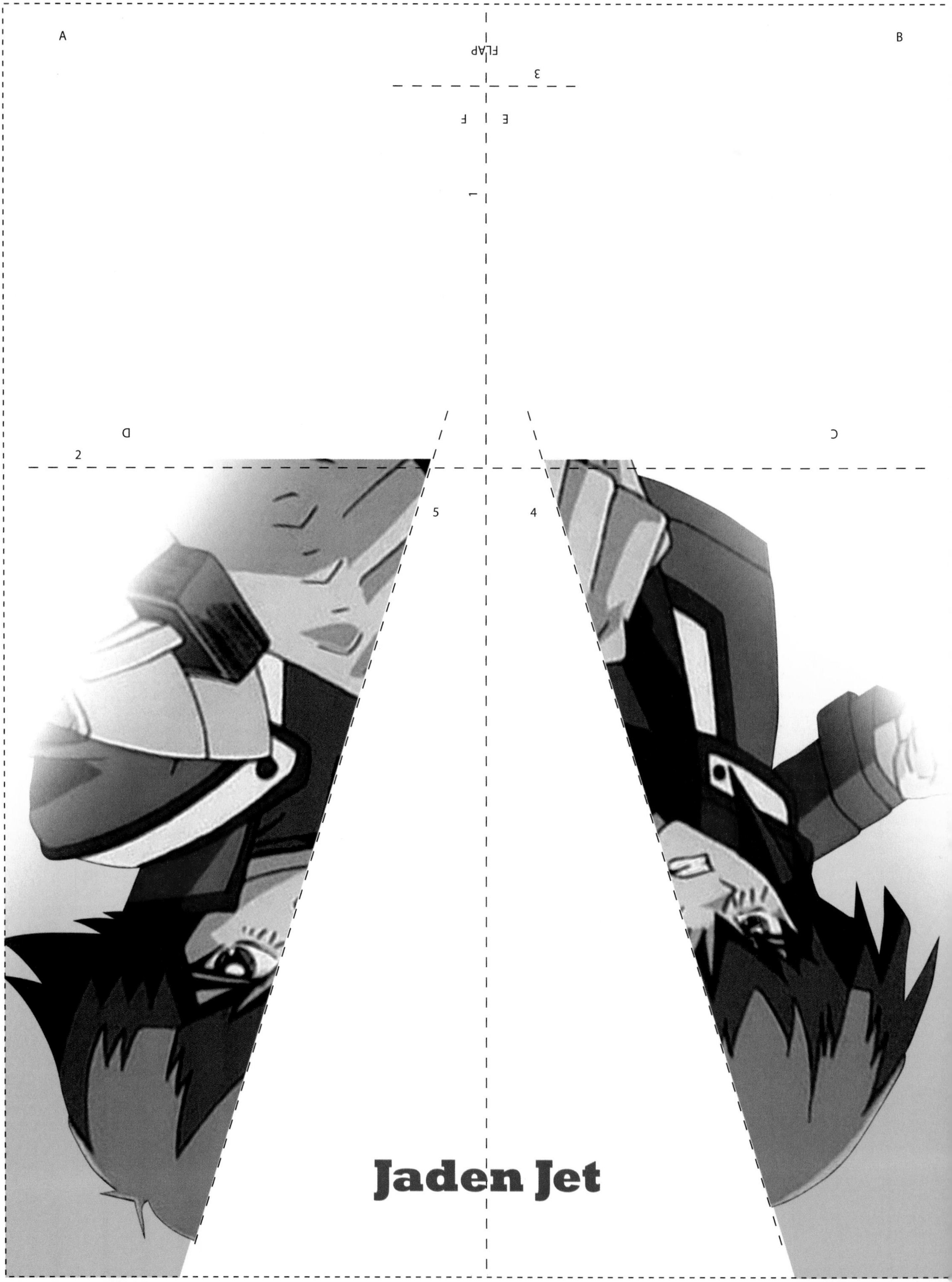
A
B
FLAP
3
E
F
1
D
C
2
5
4
Jaden Jet

GX

TRIPLE PLAY

YOU CAN COUNT ON ME

Or can you?

Use beads or coins to keep track of your life points.

10,000	1,000	100
9,000	900	90
8,000	800	80
7,000	700	70
6,000	600	60
5,000	500	50
4,000	400	40
3,000	300	30
2,000	200	20
1,000	100	10

pojo.com

When it's not just a game!